T0017567

THE LITTLE BOOK OF
BONSAI

Japanese black pine

An Easy Guide to Caring
for Your Bonsai Tree

THE LITTLE BOOK OF

BONSAI

JONAS DUPUICH

Photography by David Fenton

TEN SPEED PRESS
California | New York

CONTENTS

Coast redwood

Gray-bark elm

PREFACE

The first time I saw a small tree become a bonsai, I was hooked.

I was working at the family business, a retail nursery, when an acquaintance offered to "style" a neglected pine. He took the tree home and returned it a few days later. I could tell it was the same tree, but the pruning and wiring had completely changed its character. I wanted to learn more.

The acquaintance, Boon Manakitivipart, became my friend and teacher. I quickly joined a bonsai club and started collecting small trees. They didn't all fare well at first, but over time I learned to keep them healthy.

Learning to style the trees took longer. Were I not lucky enough to have a good teacher, I'm not sure I would have stuck with it.

For the next few years, I spent more and more time working with bonsai. I started visiting bonsai exhibits around the country and eventually began a bonsai blog to share what I learned. I found that I like writing about bonsai and have written more than a thousand posts to date.

Today I have the good fortune to work with bonsai full-time, teaching classes and growing bonsai in Northern California. When I get the chance, I travel to Japan to visit bonsai exhibitions, bonsai gardens, and the nurseries of fellow bonsai professionals.

My aim in writing this book is to help you keep your bonsai healthy and make your trees beautiful. It's the book I wish I had when I started. I hope you enjoy it!

BONSAI STYLE

It's easy to recognize a bonsai when you see one. A bonsai (pronounced "bone-sigh") is a small tree in a pot (*bonsai* means "tray planting" in Japanese). If you're interested in creating one of your own, a good first step is understanding what goes into bonsai design. To help you get started, I'll describe where bonsai come from and what makes a bonsai look like a bonsai. I'll also introduce basic bonsai styles and help you identify the most attractive features of your tree.

Where Bonsai Come From

Almost any plant that produces woody growth in the form of trunks and branches can become a bonsai. Trees, shrubs, and some vines can be trained as bonsai by pruning, wiring, and repotting—the fundamental bonsai techniques.

Some bonsai are trained from the time they are cuttings or seedlings. Others are dug up from the mountains (like the Sierra juniper pictured at left) or from garden landscapes as mature trees. Whether a tree started its life in a nursery or in the mountains, bonsai training techniques are largely the same.

Bonsai reflect their relationship with the people who care for them, as bonsai growers leave their mark on the trees under their care. Over time, the evidence of these interactions give bonsai their unique and unmistakable character.

What Makes a Bonsai Look like a Bonsai?

The defining characteristic of bonsai is their size. Bonsai are small trees, no more than three to four feet tall, which are trained in the form of much larger trees growing in nature.

Although bonsai resemble full-size trees, they are not exact copies in miniature. Bonsai resemble idealized versions of mature trees with lots of character.

Old trees grow slowly and produce fine branches, thick bark, and prominent roots that are visible at the base of the trunk. The crown of the tree is rounded, as in the Korean hornbeam at right, unlike the pointy tops of younger trees.

Like mature trees in nature, bonsai are roughly triangular in shape. This is a result of lower branches extending further from the trunk than the upper branches in order to capture sunlight.

How one interprets the idea of a mature tree differs from person to person and provides a wonderful diversity of bonsai forms around the world.

A Coast redwood

B Spruce

C Japanese maple

Basic Bonsai Styles

Trees with similar characteristics can be grouped into bonsai styles that are based on the shape or character of the trunk, roots, and branches. Some of the most basic styles are defined by the shape of the trunk.

In a formal upright bonsai, the trunk grows straight up (see A, facing page). This is the predominant shape of forest trees such as redwoods, firs, larches, and cryptomeria.

In an informal upright bonsai (see photos, pages 7 and 83), the trunk rises upward with gentle curves. This is one of the most common forms used in bonsai. Maples, junipers, and pines are frequently grown in this style.

In a slant style bonsai, the trunk is relatively straight but grows at an angle (see B, facing page). This style evokes trees in nature that grow under the influence of strong winds or reach to one side to seek out sunlight. Almost any species of tree can be styled as a slant style bonsai.

In a semi-cascade bonsai, the trunk grows out to one side and begins to curve downward, resembling a tree that grows on a steep slope or mountainside (see C, facing page).

In a cascade bonsai, the trunk follows a similar pattern but grows further downward (see photo, page 3).

The two cascading styles differ by how far down the trunk grows. The trunks on semi-cascade bonsai bend slightly downward but grow primarily out to the side. The trunks of cascade bonsai grow primarily downward beyond the bottom of the pot.

Bonsai can be styled in many other forms, some of which have more than one trunk:

→ Twin-trunk bonsai have two trunks (see A, facing page).

→ Triple-trunk bonsai have three trunks.

→ Bonsai with more than five trunks are called multitrunk or clump style bonsai (see B, facing page).

Other styles are defined by the general character of the tree:

→ Literati or *bunjin* ("literary person") style bonsai have slender trunks with subtle but interesting movement and sparse branches (see C, facing page). These bonsai evoke slow-growing trees with great age.

→ Driftwood or *yamadori* ("taken from the mountains") style bonsai feature dramatic deadwood. Dead branches (*jin*) and dead wood along the trunk (*shari*) become features that convey the tree's experience growing in a harsh environment, where it's natural for branches or sections of the trunk to die back (see photo, page 4).

→ Windswept bonsai resemble trees that grow in environments characterized by strong winds. The trunk and branches on windswept bonsai can take a variety of shapes but predominantly extend to one direction or the other.

A Stewartia

B Ginkgo

C Japanese black pine

Trident maple

Some bonsai styles are defined by the character of the roots:

→ A root-over-rock bonsai grows on top of a stone, with roots that spread over the stone and into the soil (see photo, above).

→ Exposed root bonsai evoke trees growing where the soil has eroded, with roots exposed to the elements (see upper photo, facing page).

Compositions with more than one bonsai in the same pot are known as forest style bonsai or group plantings (see lower photo, facing page).

Japanese black pine

Japanese red pine

Finding the Front of Your Bonsai

Now that you've seen some of the forms bonsai can take, you can begin to identify styles that are appropriate for your own bonsai. Your first step will be finding the front of your tree to highlight its most attractive features. The basic approach is simple. First, evaluate the tree to become familiar with its good and bad points. Then select the side of the tree that shows off the good points and downplays the bad points. The following steps walk you through the process.

1. Evaluate the trunk.

   Some trunks have interesting curves when viewed from one side but appear relatively straight from other sides. The side with a view of the most interesting curves provides the best candidate for the front.

   If tilting the tree to one side or the other makes it more attractive, you can change the angle at which the tree is planted when you repot it (see page 67 for more about repotting).

2. Evaluate the surface roots.

   Identify the side of the tree that shows the most attractive surface roots. (If you can't see any roots, scrape away some of the soil at the base of the trunk.) Examples of unattractive surface roots include roots that emerge at awkward angles, crossing roots, and unevenly spaced roots with large gaps between them.

3. Evaluate the branches.

   A good front enables the viewer to see the trunk clearly. If one side of your tree has many branches that make it difficult to appreciate the shape of the trunk, this side is not a good candidate for the front.

   Select a side of the tree that orients the best branches to the sides to reduce the number of branches you'll have to prune or wire when you style the tree.

4. Identify special features you want to highlight.

   Beautiful bark can indicate a tree's age and character. Choose the side of the trunk with the most attractive bark for the front.

   Dead areas on the trunk (*shari*) or dead branches (*jin*) can make attractive features on species such as juniper that exhibit deadwood in nature (see photo, page 4). Orient the tree so that these features are highlighted.

5. Identify flaws you want to downplay.

   Unsightly scars are the most common example of flaws on the trunk. Try to select a front that doesn't feature them.

After you carefully review these criteria, you should have a good idea of which side of your tree should be facing front. Sometimes, many of the best features of a tree are on the same side as the least interesting features. In this case, select the side that you like best and try to downplay the flaws as you make improvements to the trunk, roots, and branches over time.

SIDE A

Here's an example based on two views of the same tree (shore pine).

The owner of this tree selected side A for the front. If you compare the shape of the trunk in these photos, the trunk looks relatively straight on side B but reveals curves on side A. Branches obscure

SIDE B

the middle section of the trunk on side B, whereas side A provides a good view of this area. Side A also offers of a view of a dead branch, or *jin*, on the right side of the trunk, which is a desirable trait.

CARING FOR YOUR BONSAI

With proper care and nourishment, your bonsai can stay healthy for a long time. Even if you are new to growing bonsai, you can learn to provide your tree with the sunlight, water, and fertilizer it needs to stay healthy, and recognize when it is troubled by pests or disease.

Plum

Selecting an Appropriate Environment for Your Tree

When you're deciding where to grow a bonsai, one of your most important considerations is whether it will grow better indoors or outdoors. Many popular bonsai species prefer growing outdoors, including most conifers and deciduous bonsai, as well as broadleaf evergreen species. If your bonsai is a juniper, pine, elm, maple, oak, or azalea, it will likely grow best outside.

Bonsai such as ficus and Brazilian rain trees are native to tropical climates. If you live in a region with hot and humid weather, tropical bonsai will grow best outdoors. If it's cooler where you live, these bonsai will grow better indoors where it's warmer. In general, keep tropical bonsai inside when the outdoor temperature regularly drops below 50°F.

The basics of keeping bonsai healthy indoors are simple:

→ Ensure that growing spaces have bright, indirect light.

→ Avoid placing bonsai in spaces that receive direct sunlight through closed windows. Without the cooling effect of fresh air, the heat of the sun can burn foliage (see photo, page 33).

→ Avoid placing bonsai near heating vents where hot air can dry out trees quickly.

It may take a few attempts to identify an ideal location for bonsai in your home. Try experimenting by growing your bonsai in different locations and see what works best.

Outdoor bonsai need at least three to four hours of sunlight each day. In mild climates, your outdoor tree may grow well in direct sunlight. Conifers such as junipers and pines commonly grow in full sun, while deciduous varieties such as maples and elms prefer growing where they get some shade.

Common Indoor Bonsai

Brazilian rain tree	jaboticaba	serissa
ficus	jade	
fukien tea	schefflera	

Common Outdoor Bonsai

azalea	gardenia	persimmon
bald cypress	ginkgo	pine
beech	grape	plum
bougainvillea	hemlock	podocarpus
boxwood	hinoki cypress	pomegranate
camellia	hornbeam	quince
cedar	Japanese maple	redwood
Chinese elm	juniper	spruce
crabapple	magnolia	stewartia
cryptomeria	oak	trident maple
flowering apricot (ume)	olive	wisteria

Jade

Do note, however, that there can be a big difference between sunny days in Seattle, Washington, and Dallas, Texas. Regularly checking for signs that your bonsai is getting too little or too much sunlight will help you make sure your bonsai receives the right amount.

Look for these signs that your bonsai is not getting enough sunlight:

→ The foliage changes color. Insufficient light can make foliage turn a dark shade of green before fading to a pale gray or yellow.

→ The tree drops foliage without wilting. Too much time in the dark can cause your tree to lose leaves.

→ The new growth is leggy. Leaves increase in size and the gaps between leaves lengthen to the point where new shoots look flimsy or stretched out.

→ The tree stops growing. Bonsai that don't get enough sunlight can't produce new growth.

If you see any of these signs, move your tree to a spot with more sunlight. For indoor trees, you can move a tree closer to a window, even if it means that the tree will receive some direct sunlight. For outdoor trees, move the tree to a different part of the garden, or elevate the tree on a bench or pedestal.

Look for these signs that your bonsai is getting too much sunlight:

→ The tree wilts easily and recovers slowly. Too much sunlight can be stressful for bonsai and prevents leaves from functioning properly.

→ The tree develops sunburned or discolored foliage. Pale yellow or brown patches on foliage that faces the sun clearly indicate that the tree is getting too much sunlight (see photo, page 33).

→ The tree drops leaves. Too much heat or sun can cause a tree to wilt, discolor, and lose leaves after a hot day.

If you see signs that your tree is getting too much sunlight, try moving it to a location that receives less sunlight during the hottest part of the day. If the temperature regularly gets above 90°F, protect your bonsai from the afternoon sun by placing it in a shady corner of your garden to prevent foliage from burning.

Bonsai are just as sensitive to excessive cold as they are to excessive heat. If winter temperatures where you live drop below freezing for more than twenty-four hours at a time, you may need to shelter your trees from the cold. Placing outside bonsai next to the house or under an eave can provide a break from the cold and reduce exposure to the wind. Protect bonsai from severe cold spells by placing them in a greenhouse heated to just above freezing or in a corner of the garage. If shelter is unavailable, place bonsai on the ground and add mulch around the pot to insulate the roots.

In fall and spring, sudden cold snaps can damage your bonsai—particularly in spring, when unexpected frost or hail can damage new foliage.

As the seasons change, you may find that sunny spaces become shady or shady spaces become sunny. Move your bonsai throughout the year to ensure that they receive the best amount of sun or shade. If you rotate your bonsai 180 degrees each month, each side of the tree will receive equal amounts of sunlight over time.

How to Water Bonsai Effectively

Once you've found the right environment for your tree, the number one thing you can do to keep it healthy is to develop good watering habits. The best way to determine whether your bonsai needs water is to investigate the soil. If you are familiar with the soil your tree grows in, you can use your eyes as an initial gauge of dryness; dry soil is often a lighter color than wet soil (see photo, facing page).

To gauge the moisture level below the surface, use your finger or a chopstick to poke down where the roots are growing. If the soil in the top third of the pot is mostly dry, it is time to water.

Water your bonsai the same way you water other container plants in your home or garden. If you grow bonsai indoors, hold the tree under a spigot or dunk your bonsai in a basin filled with water. Outside, provide water using a watering can or a hose-end nozzle with a gentle setting.

Continue watering until water emerges from the pot's drainage holes. Your goal is to moisten all of the soil in the pot, and then give the soil time to partially dry out before you water again. Don't worry about giving a tree too much water at any one time, because the excess water will drain out of the pot's drainage holes.

It's also okay to wet the leaves when you water. Watering the foliage is good for bonsai because it washes away dust and insects and cools trees on hot days.

Watering Bonsai Throughout the Year

Bonsai have different watering needs at different times of the year. To keep your bonsai healthy, your watering habits may need to change with the seasons. This is particularly true in winter when bonsai go dormant. Dormancy is a rest period for trees characterized by reduced metabolism and suspended growth. Most conifers and broadleaf evergreens retain their foliage when they are dormant, whereas deciduous trees lose their leaves.

Bonsai experiencing winter dormancy may need water only once a week. In summer, the same tree may need water every day. It's common for bonsai to need more water on hot days, windy days, or during times of the year when the tree is growing quickly. Bonsai that are weak or unhealthy typically require less water.

Checking the soil regularly is the best way to ensure that your tree is getting the right amount of water throughout the year. If your bonsai wilts on days you don't water, try watering more frequently.

Here are signs that your bonsai needs more water:

→ The foliage wilts.

→ Leaves become dry and crispy.

It may come as a surprise to learn that watering trees too frequently is just as problematic as not watering frequently enough. Roots growing in waterlogged soil may die because they can't absorb the oxygen they need. To prevent overwatering, make sure the soil is partially dry before you water.

Shimpaku juniper

Here are signs that your bonsai needs less water:

→ The soil never dries out.

→ The soil smells rotten.

→ Foliage becomes limp without drying out.

→ The tips of the leaves turn brown. This can also be caused by underwatering, so check to see if the soil is wet or dry to determine the cause of the damage.

And here are additional watering tips:

→ If a decorative top dressing such as rocks covers the surface of the soil, it can be hard to tell when your bonsai needs water. Remove the top dressing to make it easier to keep your bonsai properly watered.

→ Water early in the day to prepare your bonsai for the afternoon heat and to give the soil and foliage time to dry before evening.

→ Good drainage is important for all bonsai. If it takes more than a minute for water to drain through the soil when you water, consider repotting the tree at the next available opportunity. (See page 67 for more about repotting.)

→ Some bonsai are planted in containers without drainage holes. If this is the case for your bonsai, drill holes in the bottom of the container or repot the tree into a container that facilitates drainage as soon as possible.

→ If you're leaving town for a few days, find someone to care for your trees to ensure they don't dry out while you're away.

→ If you have more than one bonsai, check the soil of each tree before watering as different species have different watering needs. Deciduous species, for example, typically require more frequent watering than conifers.

Fertilizer Basics

Bonsai get the bulk of their nutrition from a combination of sunlight, water, and air. Daily watering and fresh air provide bonsai with ample amounts of the carbon, hydrogen, and oxygen they need to produce their own food. They get the rest of their nutrients from the soil. As bonsai grow, however, they deplete the available resources in the soil. You can replenish these resources by adding fertilizer. Fertilizing bonsai can improve tree health, encourage new growth, and help trees respond to training. The most common signs that bonsai need fertilizer are yellow foliage and weak or stunted growth.

Plastic covers keep these organic fertilizer pellets in place

If you are new to fertilizing bonsai, here are some tips for getting started:

→ The most important nutrients to look for in fertilizers are nitrogen, phosphorus, and potassium (N-P-K). The three bold numbers on fertilizer labels indicate the amount of these elements by weight. For example, a 5-5-5 fertilizer is 5 percent nitrogen, 5 percent phosphorus, and 5 percent potassium. Fertilizers with up to 5 percent to 6 percent of each nutrient are good for bonsai.

→ Some fertilizers are liquid, such as fish emulsion, and others are solid, such as cottonseed meal. Both types work well for bonsai, so you can select the type that is most convenient for you to apply. Note that fish emulsion, which is great for outdoor bonsai, can smell fishy, so it may not be appropriate for indoor bonsai.

→ Organic fertilizers are a good choice because they support the bacteria and fungi that break down organic matter in the soil and make nutrients available to your bonsai. They also improve the soil's ability to hold air and water, which helps keep roots healthy.

Consult the instructions on the label to determine how much fertilizer to use and how frequently to use it. If there are no instructions for applying the fertilizer on container-grown trees, start with half of the recommended application rate and check to see how the tree responds over the next two to three weeks. If the tree continues to look healthy, try working up to the full application rate over subsequent applications.

Alternatively, if you notice that the edges of the leaves turn brown or the tree no longer dries out between water applications, it may have absorbed too much fertilizer. To help it recover, remove

excess fertilizer from the surface of the soil and hold off on future applications until the tree regains its health.

Here are a few fertilizer application tips:

→ Start fertilizing bonsai in early spring and continue until the first hard freeze in fall or winter. If you live in a mild climate, continue fertilizing through fall.

→ Apply fertilizer lightly on bonsai that are weak or unhealthy as sick trees don't use as much fertilizer as healthy trees.

→ Don't apply fertilizer during periods of excessive heat or cold. In winter, avoid fertilizing when the temperature drops below freezing. In summer, avoid fertilizing on the hottest days of the year.

Common Pests and Diseases

Just like people, bonsai occasionally get sick. Some illnesses are easy to spot while others require more effort to pin down. If you suspect your tree isn't healthy, avoid pruning or wiring, because this can further stress your tree.

Identifying the Problem

Check bonsai foliage by inspecting the upper and lower leaf surfaces. Look closely at the branches and trunk. If you are repotting the bonsai, check the soil and roots. If you see any of the following symptoms, your next step is to identify the cause:

→ Discolored foliage or stems that look yellow, brown, or gray

→ Spotted or splotchy foliage

→ Fuzzy growth on leaf surfaces

→ Dead leaves on otherwise healthy branches

→ Malformed or missing sections of foliage

→ Foliage that has been rolled or folded

→ Visible insects on foliage, stems, or roots

→ Dead roots (roots that appear limp, desiccated, or dark inside and out)

The most common culprits for these symptoms are pests, fungi, and bacteria.

Common Pests and Controls

Pests such as insects, snails, and slugs can range in size, from easy to spot to microscopic. Here are some common pests that attack bonsai and first steps you can take to remove them from your trees:

→ Aphids are sucking insects that feed on sap from leaves, stems, and roots. You'll often see them in clusters of black, white, green, or yellow dots (see photo, facing page). Treat minor infestations by removing the insects with a cloth or washing them off with water.

→ Scale are a diverse group of insects that resemble small dots or bumps on leaves or stems (see photo, facing page). They can be barely perceptible or up to a quarter-inch in size, flat or rounded in shape, and black, brown, or white in color. Pick off large scale by hand. Treat minor scale infestations by spraying affected trees with insecticidal soap or horticultural oil.

→ Mealybugs are white insects often found in cottony masses. They prefer warm, humid environments. Like aphids, they feed on sap and produce honeydew, a sweet excretion that can lead to sooty mold (see photo, facing page). Treatment is similar to treatment for aphids and scale.

Spider mite damage
on shimpaku juniper

Pine needle scale on
Japanese black pine

Aphids on wisteria

Sunburned foliage on
Norfolk Island pine

Thrips damage on azalea

Sooty mold on oleander

→ Whiteflies are small white winged insects that feed on sap. They are a common pest on indoor bonsai. Because whiteflies can quickly develop resistance to pesticides, nontoxic controls such as insecticidal soaps and horticultural oils are good options for treatment.

→ Thrips are tiny black or brown insects commonly found on azalea bonsai. Foliage damaged by thrips is often splotchy and gray or silver in color, particularly on the leaf undersides (see photo, page 33). Azalea lace bugs (small insects with translucent, lace like wings) can cause similar damage. Insecticidal soaps and horticultural oils are effective controls for both pests.

→ Spider mites resemble specs of dust to the naked eye. They reproduce quickly and thrive in hot, dry conditions. In pines and junipers, look for tiny yellow dots that give foliage a gray or yellow cast (see photo, page 33). Overhead watering is the best way to prevent spider mite infestations.

→ Caterpillars are larval butterflies or moths that feed on leaves. They are often well-camouflaged. Although they can be quite destructive, you can control them by spraying biological pesticides such as *Bacillus thuringiensis* (Bt) on the foliage.

→ Snails and slugs eat tender foliage and leave behind silver trails. Removing them by hand is the best way to keep your bonsai free from these pests.

→ Ants often invade plants when other insects are residing on your bonsai, particularly aphids, mealybugs, and scale, because ants like to eat the honeydew excreted by these insects. If you see ants on your trees, look for other pests. Getting rid of the pests will usually get rid of the ants.

A good approach to treating pests is to start with the least toxic controls and work up to stronger alternatives as needed. Keep in mind that not all controls are appropriate for every pest. Follow the instructions on the product label to ensure that you are using pest controls effectively.

Physical damage on privet caused by leaves bumping into a fence

Fungus damage on valley oak

Powdery mildew on hydrangea

Fungus damage on live oak

Fungus damage on rose

Common Diseases Caused by Fungi or Bacteria

If insects aren't responsible for the symptoms you find on your bonsai, fungi or bacteria may be the cause. Here are some of the most common fungi and diseases that attack bonsai:

→ Powdery mildew is a fungus that looks like fuzzy white spots or patches on the surface of leaves (see photo, page 35). If untreated, it can damage or discolor leaves. Home remedies such as milk sprays (solutions of 1 part milk and 2 parts water, sprayed on affected foliage) can be effective against powdery mildew.

→ Rust is an orange-colored fungus that grows on leaf surfaces. Remove affected foliage and reduce overhead watering to treat minor cases.

→ Sooty mold is a fungus that grows on honeydew excreted by aphids, mealybugs, scale, and other insects that feed on sap. It is usually dark gray or black in color and can resemble a coating of dirt or dust on the foliage (see photo, page 33). Treating the underlying insect infestation will usually clear up the sooty mold.

→ Root rot can be caused by a number of diseases, including pythium, phytophthora, and armillaria. Signs that a bonsai may have root rot include unexpected declines in health, poor growth, dieback, and pale foliage. Affected roots appear dark, limp, or desiccated. Poor soil and too much moisture are the primary causes of root rot diseases. Removing dead roots during repotting and using soil that allows for good drainage is the best protection against root rot.

As with controlling pests, a good approach to treating disease is to start with the least toxic controls and work up to stronger alternatives as needed.

Pest and Disease Prevention and Tips

Here are some tips for working with unhealthy or infested bonsai:

→ Damaged foliage generally doesn't heal. If an insect has chewed leaves or a fungus has left behind spots, these symptoms will likely remain after the underlying problem is addressed. In time, damaged foliage will fall away and be replaced by healthy foliage.

→ When you use contact sprays such as insecticidal soaps, oils, or pesticides, coat all surfaces of foliage well. Skipping the undersides of leaves, for example, can provide shelter for insects or fungi and make treatment ineffective.

→ When you're working with diseased foliage, sterilize your tools between cuts by cleaning the blades with alcohol or bleach to prevent spreading fungi or bacteria to other parts of the tree.

→ If you need help identifying a pest or disease, take a sample in a sealed plastic bag to a local nursery or garden center.

One of the most important things you can do to keep your trees healthy is to avoid conditions that favor pests and disease from taking hold in your garden:

→ Avoid overwatering and overfertilizing.

→ Thin crowded foliage to reduce hiding places for insects.

→ Avoid placing your bonsai near infested trees in the garden.

→ Keep bonsai foliage clean by overhead watering.

→ If you have more than a few trees, provide adequate space between them so that each gets sunlight and fresh air.

→ Protect bonsai from excessive heat or cold to avoid stress caused by extreme temperatures.

Over time, you will become familiar with the problems that affect bonsai in your area and the most effective treatments. With proper care, your bonsai will stay healthy and be ready for the artistic work you have planned for it.

CHAPTER III

TOOLS AND TECHNIQUES

In this chapter, I'll describe tools that are designed for working with bonsai and introduce the fundamental techniques of pruning and wiring you'll use to style your tree. With some practice, these tools and techniques will become a natural part of your overall approach to bonsai.

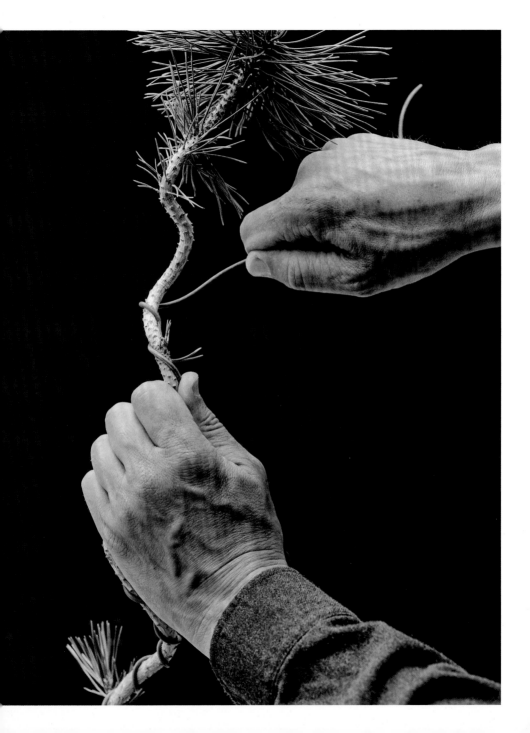

Tools

If you use tools in the garden or around the house, you can use these to work with your bonsai. Over time, you can acquire tools made specifically for bonsai that are designed to help you work quickly and comfortably.

Basic Bonsai Tools

→ Bonsai **scissors** are available in a variety of styles. Scissors with slender tips are designed for removing young shoots or small branches. Heavy-duty shears are made for removing larger branches.

→ **Branch cutters**, or concave cutters, are used for shortening or removing branches. The angle of the cutting blades enables you to cut branches in hard-to-reach places.

→ Bonsai **wire cutters** have blunt tips for cutting wire away from branches without damaging the bark. They are especially helpful when you're working with thicker wires.

→ Bonsai **pliers** have narrow, rounded tips for working in small spaces without damaging branch tissue. They are useful for reaching where your fingers don't fit when applying or removing bonsai wire, and they can help apply leverage when you're bending wired branches.

→ **Tweezers** are useful for removing dead leaves or plucking pine needles. Bent-nose models are helpful for removing old soil from roots during repotting.

Wire cutters

Concave branch cutter

Scissors

Pilers

Tweezers

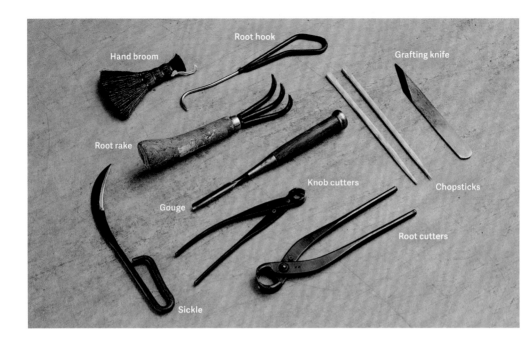

Beyond the Basics

As you improve your bonsai skills, you may add several specialized tools to your toolbox:

→ **Knob cutters** have rounded blades for gouging out wood left behind by branch cutters. The concave shape of the cut helps trees form a smooth callus over the cut area.

→ **Root cutters** are similar to branch or knob cutters but are designed for cutting larger roots.

→ Small **sickles** are repotting tools for separating roots from the sides of the pot. If a tree is rootbound and hasn't been repotted in several years, a sickle can make it easier to remove the tree from the pot.

- → **Woodworking chisels, gouges, and knives** are great for creating deadwood features such as *jin* on branches or *shari* along the trunk.

- → Use a small **hand broom** to clean the surface of the soil after pruning or repotting bonsai or to clean up your work area.

- → **Root hooks and rakes** can help comb away soil from the roots during repotting.

- → Use **chopsticks** during repotting for gently combing old soil away from the roots or for removing air pockets when adding new soil.

- → **Cut paste** is putty or paste designed to seal wounds and stimulate callus formation.

Pruning

Although there are many reasons to prune bonsai, the most important are to improve the shape of the tree, to refine the branch structure, and to promote budding in the tree's interior. When you first style your bonsai, you'll make some cuts to establish the overall size and shape of the tree. Over time, your tree may grow beyond this size and shape. By pruning, you can reestablish your design and keep your tree small.

Pruning can help you refine the branch structure when you remove unattractive branches. At the same time, pruning helps promote budding in the tree's interior as it lets more light into the tree's interior, which stimulates new growth.

Bar branches

Shoot growing from an intersection between two branches

Branch whorl

Branch growing straight down

Identifying Branches to Prune

One of the easiest ways to start pruning your bonsai is to identify faulty branch patterns. Here are some of the most common.

→ Bar branches are two branches that emerge from opposite sides of the trunk creating a strong horizontal line, or bar shape. Consider removing one of the two branches.

→ Branch intersections are most attractive when a large branch cleanly divides into two. Remove any new shoots that sprout from established branch intersections.

→ A whorl occurs when many branches emerge from the same spot. Whorls can cause unattractive swelling or a knuckle to form along the trunk. To avoid this, reduce the number of branches that emerge from a single point.

→ Vertical growth can detract from the design of your tree. Prune (or wire) branches that grow straight up or straight down.

These patterns are some of the most common examples of faulty branching on bonsai, but you'll likely spot others as well. If a branch is unattractive and doesn't contribute to the overall design of the tree, feel free to remove it. You may, however, find that every branch on your tree fits into one of these faulty categories. In this case, remove the least attractive branches and use the remaining branches to create your design.

Timing of Pruning

The best times to prune bonsai are at the beginning of the growing season (just before buds open in spring), the middle of the growing season (typically May or June), and the end of the growing season when bonsai start to go dormant in fall.

How to Prune

Identify a branch to cut. The branch on the left is distracting because it is straight. Removing it is the best option to improve the tree because the branch is too thick to bend with wire.

Carefully start the cut where the branch emerges from the trunk.

If your tools are in good condition, you will have a nice, clean cut with no ragged edges.

After you remove the branch, treat the wound with cut paste to promote callus formation.

Wiring

One of the easiest ways to make bonsai more attractive is to arrange the branches using wire. It's also one of the fastest ways to make improvements, because it takes less time to reposition a branch than it does to grow a new one.

The two most popular wire choices for bonsai are anodized aluminum and annealed copper. For small trees under 12 inches tall, wire sizes between 1.5 mm and 3.0 mm (aluminum) or between 16 gauge and 12 gauge (copper) are useful. Bending branches on larger trees often requires thicker wires ranging from 2.0 mm to 5.0 mm (aluminum) or from 14 gauge to 8 gauge (copper).

Aluminum wire is softer than copper, which makes it easier to apply. Annealed copper is stronger than aluminum, giving it more holding power and making it a popular choice for larger trees or trees with big branches that need bending.

How to Apply Bonsai Wire

Wiring a branch requires preparing the branch for wiring, planning a path for the wire to follow, and applying the wire. To prepare a branch for wiring, first notice any leaves or small branches along the paths you want to wire and remove them to ensure that the wire makes good contact with the branch.

The branch shown in the image above splits into three smaller branches. All the foliage grows near the end of the branch, so there is no need for additional preparation.

The three branches can be shaped with two pieces of wire. The first wire will secure the main line of the branch, and the second wire will connect the two smaller branches. To apply the wire, use one hand to hold the wire close against the branch and the other hand to wrap the wire around the branch, one spiral at a time, moving from the base of the branch to the tip (see photo, page 39).

The next wire will connect the two smaller branches. When wiring two branches with a single piece of wire, select branches that are similar in size and located close to each other. Begin by positioning the middle of the wire at the base of the lower branch to be wired. Apply the wire outward from this intersection toward the end of each branch you are wiring.

Once all the branches have been wired, use both hands to bend the branches gently into shape. Start by adding curves to straight branches, making small adjustments until you are satisfied with the branch shapes.

Here are some tips for setting, or bending, wired branches:

→ If you created gaps in the foliage after pruning, bend branches into position to fill the gaps.

→ Try to make the branch angles consistent from top to bottom. For conifers, it's common to bend branches downward, as the branches on mature conifers tend to point downward as they age. For deciduous trees, branches generally rise up and out (see photo, page 79).

→ If you plan to wire all of the branches on your tree, begin with the lowest branches and work your way up to the top. Set the largest branches first and then set the smaller branches at similar angles.

→ For more refined trees, particularly conifers, you can create *branch pads*, blocks of foliage comprising one or more smaller branches. Line up smaller branches to create the branch pad shape (see lower left photo, page 85).

Common Wiring Mistakes

The best way to improve your wiring is to correct mistakes when you see them. Here are some of the most common wiring mistakes and tips for correcting them:

→ Uneven spirals. These are unsightly and ineffective. Apply wire with consistent spirals between 55 and 60 degrees

→ Gaps between the wire and the branch. Bonsai wire works best when it's close-fitting, but not too tight, against the branch. To avoid gaps, hold the wire snugly against the branch with one hand while applying the wire with the other.

→ Crossed wires. When one wire crosses another, it puts pressure on the lower wire, which can damage the bark as the tree grows. Try connecting different pairs of branches to avoid crossing wires.

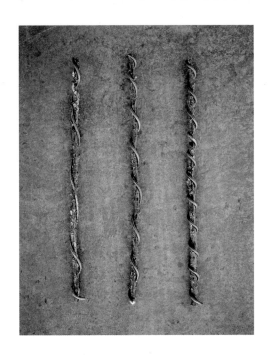

→ More than three wires in a single location. Avoid routing more than three wires through the same intersection. To fix this, select different pairs of branches to wire to make your wiring more attractive.

→ Teeter-totter branches. Branches are said to teeter-totter when bending one wired branch causes another branch to move. This is common when wiring two branches that emerge at the same point along the trunk. Try connecting two branches that emerge from the trunk at least one inch away from each other.

→ Wire is too thin. If a wire isn't strong enough to hold a branch in place after bending it, remove the wire and use a thicker wire. Having different sizes of wire on hand will make it easier to find the right size wire for each branch.

→ Spirals that are too long or too short. In the photo above, the spirals on the left are too far apart, the ones on the right are too close together, and the ones in the center are just right.

Wiring Follow-up

Bonsai wire isn't a permanent fixture on your tree. As a wired branch grows, the bends you create will begin to hold their shape. Once this new shape is set, you can remove the wire.

If you remove the wire before the bend sets, the branch will return to its original position. If you leave the wire in place too long, it can cut into the bark, creating unsightly swelling or scarring as in the photo at right. Some scarring is okay on conifers, because the branches are often hidden by the foliage, but scarring is less desirable on deciduous species because the branches are visible in winter.

Wire can begin to cut into the bark after one or two months on fast-growing trees. On slower growing trees, you can keep the wire in place for a year or two without damaging the branch. Check your bonsai regularly to ensure that the wire is not cutting into the bark.

It's easy to remove small wires by hand. The process is the reverse of the one you used to apply the wire. Hold the wire tight against the branch with one hand and unwind one spiral at a time until the wire is free from the branch. Remove larger wires by carefully cutting one spiral at a time with a wire cutter. Be careful not to tear the bark if the wire has started to cut into the branch.

Initial Styling

Now that you're familiar with basic bonsai styles and techniques, you're ready to create your own bonsai. An overview of the process is on the following pages. Be sure to perform this work only on healthy trees at the right time of year for pruning (see page 45) or repotting (see page 67).

Step-by-Step Initial Styling

The shimpaku juniper shown above is an example of a prebonsai, a form in which the grower has created bends and twists in the trunk but not in the branches.

We start by finding the most attractive side of the tree. On our tree, the best curves in the trunk appear on the top half where the trunk grows to the left. To show off these curves, we can tilt the tree at a 45-degree angle to create a semi-cascade bonsai.

At this point, the front doesn't need to be exact. It's simply a guide that will help with branch selection and wiring.

Next, we prune to remove branches that aren't necessary for the tree's design and to shorten branches that are too long. For this shimpaku, we shorten the longest branches by half and remove the larger branches on the right side of the tree. Removing these branches reveals more of the trunk and makes it easier to appreciate the curves that give the tree character.

The next step is to create some deadwood features (*jin*), by using a knife to define the area where the bark will be removed and then peeling the bark away with pliers to reveal the wood underneath.

Close-up of the branch turned into a *jin*.

After the pruning and deadwood work, we wire the tree, beginning with the main branches and then the smallest branches. We wire each branch into the shape of a simple branch pad.

We don't need to wire every branch—the goal is to establish the initial design by bending the primary branches that emerge from the trunk. When the wiring is completed, the main branches point slightly down and to the left.

Now we repot the tree into a pot that's suitable for semi-cascade bonsai—a round pot, in this case.

CONTAINERS AND DISPLAY

Containers make it easy to distinguish a bonsai from a simple tree in a pot. The proportions and stylistic details of bonsai containers are unlike those of pots used for growing vegetables, flowers, or houseplants. In this chapter, I'll provide guidelines for selecting an appropriate container for your tree and step-by-step instructions for repotting it. I'll also provide tips for making your tree look its best when it's time to show it off.

Bonsai Containers

A bonsai container's most important job is to provide a suitable environment for the roots. A pot that is too shallow or too small cannot provide adequate insulation against severe weather or preserve enough moisture to support the tree's water needs.

Plastic nursery containers, terracotta pots, and wooden boxes are good choices for seedlings, cuttings, and young trees. Using a bonsai pot too early in development can restrict root growth and slow progress. Once your bonsai takes on a more mature shape, you can transplant it into a ceramic container that suits the tree's style.

Popular Bonsai and Container Combinations

A number of conventions can help you choose the most appropriate container for your tree. While useful, these conventions aren't requirements. Feel free to use the container you think looks best for your tree.

→ Unglazed containers and pots with subtle glazes are conventional choices for conifers because the color of the clay can provide good contrast to conifer foliage.

→ Glazed pots are conventional choices for deciduous bonsai. For trees with foliage that turns yellow in fall, for example, a yellow pot may not provide good contrast in autumn, but it would look great against the pale green foliage that emerges in spring.

→ Although broadleaf evergreen and tropical bonsai retain their foliage year-round, the character of these trees varies enough to make glazed or unglazed containers a good match.

→ Trees with sparse branching and slender trunks are a good match for shallow, round containers (see photo C, page 11). Unlike oval or rectangular pots that orient the viewer toward the front of the tree, round pots enable the viewer to appreciate the tree from all sides without providing a strong signal as to the preferred front.

→ Square, round, or hexagonal pots are a conventional choice for cascade and semi-cascade bonsai. Cascade pots are typically no deeper than they are wide.

→ Compositions with more than one tree in the pot look good in shallow containers that suggest a small landscape (see bottom photo, page 13). Soil mounded on top of a slab can also make a good base for group plantings.

→ Stones and slabs are among the most common alternatives to ceramic bonsai containers (see photo, page 64). They are appropriate for all species of bonsai.

Dwarf Japanese quince

Getting the Size Right

More important than choosing a style is getting the size right. Cutting roots to make the tree fit in a tiny container is stressful for the tree, and trees in small pots can dry out quickly. That said, using a pot that is too large can make a tree look small and guide the viewer's focus to the pot rather than the tree. The right-size pot focuses the viewer's attention on the tree. For example, the pot directly above is too small, the dark blue pot is too large, and the pot to the right is a good size for this dwarf pussy willow.

Japanese maple

Repotting Your Bonsai

Repotting is a fundamental bonsai technique that lets you maintain your tree's health and preserve its compact size. You can also repot bonsai to change the angle of the tree for aesthetic purposes, or to change the size or style of the container in which it is planted.

The basic practice involves removing a tree from its container, trimming the roots, and returning it to its previous container or moving it to a new one. When done correctly, repotting can help keep trees alive for dozens or, in some cases, hundreds of years.

How can you tell if your bonsai needs repotting? The most important indicator is when water fails to drain out of the pot. As trees grow, new roots break down the soil and fill the gaps of air between particles. Over time, this can reduce the amount of air in the soil and reduce drainage. If drainage is poor and the soil is firm to the touch, it's time to repot.

For most conifers and deciduous bonsai, the best time to repot is late winter or early spring. This applies to popular varieties including junipers, pines, maples, elms, oaks, and azaleas. Tropical bonsai such as ficus or schefflera respond best when repotted in late spring and summer when temperatures are warm.

A wide variety of repotting tools is available. At a minimum, you can repot your bonsai using a chopstick to loosen the soil and scissors to trim the roots. Specialized repotting tools, such as root hooks, root rakes, and root cutters, can be handy when you're repotting larger bonsai.

How to Repot

Check the underside of the pot for wires used to hold the tree in place, and cut them off.

Use a small sickle or chopstick to separate the root ball from the sides of the pot.

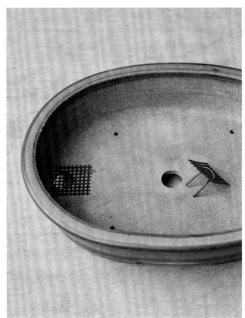

Gently remove the tree from the pot by holding the pot firmly to the table with one hand and tilting the tree to one side. Once the tree is free from the pot, carefully lift it out.

Clean the pot by gently scrubbing away any loose dirt or mineral deposits. Cover the drainage holes with plastic mesh to hold the soil in.

Insert tie-down wires to secure the tree in the pot. For pots with two or more drainage holes, cut two pieces of wire and bend them into a "U" shape. Insert the "U"-shaped wires into the drainage holes from the bottom. If your pot has one drainage hole, wrap the tie-down wire around a small section of thicker wire bent in the shape of a bobby pin and insert the tie-down wire through the bottom of the drainage hole. For trees under 12 inches tall, 2.0 mm aluminum wire is a good choice for tie-down wires. Use thicker wires for larger bonsai.

Gently scrape away soil from the top of the tree's root ball until you find the area where the trunk transitions into roots.

Remove some of the soil on the bottom and sides of the root ball.

Trim the roots so they extend from ⅛ inch to ¼ inch from the root ball.

Create a small mound of bonsai soil in the pot and nestle the root ball onto the mound of soil. Line up the surface roots with the lip of the pot.

Orient the tree so that the front of the tree aligns with the front of the pot. (For rectangular or oval pots, the front is one of the long sides.)

Connect the ends of each pair of tie-down wires by twisting them together with pliers to secure the tree into the pot. The goal is to make sure the tree doesn't move after repotting, which can damage new roots.

Fill the pot with bonsai soil. A popular bonsai soil mix consists of equal parts pumice, scoria, and akadama, a claylike particle mined in Japan. You can make your own bonsai soil by mixing these ingredients together, or you can buy premixed soil. Either way, use a sieve to remove dust before adding the soil to the pot in order to facilitate drainage.

Use a gentle jabbing motion with one or two chopsticks to incorporate new soil between the roots and remove air pockets.

Add more soil if necessary and tamp the surface of the soil until it is just below the lip of the pot.

Water the tree thoroughly. When you start to water, the water emerging from the drainage holes may be cloudy with dust. Continue watering until the water runs clear to ensure that the dust washes away.

Bonsai Display

Whether you are preparing your tree for a special occasion or for a bonsai club exhibition, a few simple steps can help you make your tree look its best.

Preparing Your Bonsai for Display

→ Remove any moss growing on the trunk or covering the surface roots. For deciduous trees with smooth bark, use a toothbrush and water to scrub away dirt or algae.

→ Prune lightly to reduce shoots that extend beyond the outline of your design and remove foliage growing on the underside of branch pads (see bottom left photo, page 85).

Moss covering the surface of the soil

→ If possible, remove all wires from the trunk and branches of deciduous bonsai. You can remove the wires on conifers if the branches will stay in position after the wires are removed.

→ Remove weeds from the pot.

→ Replace any soil that has washed out of the pot by applying a fresh layer and leveling it.

→ If moss grows in your garden, collect some with a spatula or putty knife and set it on the surface of the bonsai soil (see photo, page 73). Moss reinforces the idea that bonsai are old trees and suggests the tree's natural habitat. If you like the way moss looks on the soil, you can keep it there year-round.

→ Clean the outside of the pot by gently scrubbing away dirt or water stains. When the pot is dry, apply a thin layer of walnut, olive, or camellia oil to deepen the pot's color. Remove excess oil with a dry cloth to reduce shiny spots.

A simple bonsai display (shimpaku juniper, accent plant, and cork bark Chinese elm)

A common approach to displaying bonsai is to set the tree on a small wooden slab or table. If you have more than one tree, you can display your bonsai in a group.

It's also common to display bonsai with companion plants, known as accents or accent plants. You can use accent plants to indicate the season (for example, use flowers that bloom in spring for spring displays) or suggest the environment in which your bonsai might grow in nature (using a grass accent plant can suggest the fields in which oaks grow). Select an accent that is smaller than your tree to maintain the focus on your bonsai.

To learn more about bonsai display, visit a local bonsai exhibit or browse a bonsai exhibition book. See pages 96 and 98 for more information.

CHAPTER V

APPRECIATING DIFFERENT SPECIES

Although each bonsai species is unique, broad groups of trees share common traits. Deciduous trees, for example, often have broad canopies. By developing broad canopies in your deciduous bonsai, you can make maple or elm bonsai evoke characteristics of deciduous trees growing in nature. We can identify similar kinds of traits in other groups of trees, including coniferous, broadleaf evergreen, and tropical bonsai.

In this chapter, I'll offer tips to help you identify features to look for when shopping for bonsai, and features for you to develop based on the type of tree you are growing.

Princess persimmon

Deciduous Bonsai

Unlike most evergreens, which keep their leaves year-round, deciduous trees drop their leaves in fall when they go dormant. The defining characteristics of deciduous bonsai are revealed in winter, when you can truly appreciate the trunk and branches after the leaves have fallen. For many popular deciduous bonsai, including maples, elms, beeches, and hornbeams, the refined branch structure is the key feature of the tree.

For other deciduous species, the key features are flowers or fruit. Plums, flowering apricots, flowering quinces, and magnolias mark the start of the growing season by producing blossoms. In fall, quinces, crabapples, persimmons, and pomegranates bear colorful fruit. As a result of the changes deciduous bonsai experience throughout the year, no other bonsai mark the seasons better.

Keep the following in mind when working with deciduous bonsai:

→ The overall shapes of mature deciduous trees in nature are often broad and round, rather than slender or pointy.

→ Deciduous trunks and branches create subtle movement, whereas conifers are more likely to develop angular movement.

→ Unlike branches on conifers that grow downward, the branches on deciduous trees are more likely to grow upward (see photo A, page 11).

→ Unlike conifers, deciduous bonsai develop hard wood that can make bending trunks or larger branches difficult. Small branches can be bent, but if a branch becomes too thick to bend, removing it and growing a new one is the best way to improve the branch structure.

Cork bark Chinese elm

Key Features to Develop

→ Branch ramification. *Branch ramification* is the division of larger branches into smaller branches. You create good branch ramification through repeated pruning (see pages 43–47 for pruning guidelines).

→ Surface roots. Roots that emerge radially from the same spot along the trunk and are visible above the soil convey stability and age. You can improve surface roots when you repot by cutting roots that grow straight down and removing small roots that cross over larger roots near the surface.

→ Small leaves. Small leaves can help make a bonsai look like a full-size tree in miniature. Avoid overwatering and fertilizing heavily in spring to keep leaves small.

→ Attractive bark. Attractive bark can be a focal point of deciduous bonsai. Species such as beech and stewartia have naturally smooth bark that highlights undulations in the trunk that develop with age. Cork bark elms have craggy bark that can make relatively young trees look old.

Here are key features to look for when shopping for deciduous bonsai:

→ Attractive trunk with aged appearance

→ Good surface roots

→ Fine branches

→ Small leaves

Dwarf wisteria

Small leaves on dwarf Japanese flowering quince

Aged bark on Korean hornbeam

Coniferous Bonsai

Some of the most popular bonsai species are conifers, cone-bearing trees and shrubs that typically maintain their foliage year-round and often have slender, needlelike leaves. Conifers such as junipers, pines, spruces, hemlocks, redwoods, and firs are all good candidates for development as bonsai.

One reason for conifers' popularity is their flexibility. This flexibility helps conifers survive in extreme natural environments where they can lose their upright form and produce deformed, twisting growth. This effect, known as krummholz (from the German words for "crooked" and "wood"), can be spectacular in junipers (see photo, page 4).

Living in extreme natural environments can also cause branches or sections of the trunk to die off while the rest of the tree continues to grow. These dead areas of the tree can serve as supports for the live sections, resulting in beautiful combinations of live and dead wood, prized by bonsai enthusiasts.

Key Features to Develop

→ Refined branch pads. Refined branch pads reflect long-term development in conifer bonsai. A *branch pad* is a block of foliage made up of one or more smaller branches. The pad shape resembles blocks of foliage on full-size conifers growing in nature.

→ Twisting movement and deadwood. These features are valuable in all conifers but are particularly prized in juniper bonsai as they define junipers that grow in harsh environments. Juniper wood is flexible, and the trunk and branches can be bent and curved for dramatic effects.

→ Aged bark. Mature pines, firs, and spruce convey their age through their bark. When you're working with old bonsai specimens, avoid handling the trunk to preserve the flaky plates of bark.

→ Good surface roots. Strong roots that emerge near the surface of the soil provide stability and convey age.

Here are key features to look for when shopping for conifers:

→ Attractive trunks with good bark and natural movement

→ Good distribution of branches (evenly spaced from top to bottom, emerging from all sides of the trunk)

→ Interesting deadwood features

→ Short, straight needles (pines)

→ Good surface roots

Aged bark on a shore pine

Branch pads on a shimpaku juniper

Deadwood feature on a Sierra juniper

Broadleaf Evergreen Bonsai

Broadleaf evergreen trees and shrubs have flat leaves and maintain their foliage year-round. Mature specimens in nature often have wide, spreading canopies supported by long, undulating branches. Popular broadleaf evergreen species trained as bonsai include boxwood, live oaks, hollies, olives, and azaleas.

Some species, like boxwood or yaupon holly, grow shrublike in nature and lack characteristic forms suitable for bonsai. One option for styling these trees is to take design cues from species like oak that naturally grow in shapes that work well for bonsai.

Other broadleaf evergreens, like camellias or azaleas, are grown primarily for their flowers. Young specimens can be trained with tall, slender trunks and horizontal branches to show off as many flowers as possible.

Key Features to Develop

→ Dense foliage. Dense, dark green foliage conveys health in broadleaf evergreen bonsai. Proper sunlight, water, and fertilizer encourage healthy foliage.

→ Trunks and branches with undulating movement. If you are working with young material, wire the trunks and branches early to create movement that looks natural. Cut straight branches that are too rigid to bend.

→ Broad canopy with a rounded apex. As your broadleaf evergreen bonsai grows, let the foliage fill in to create the rounded forms mature trees take in nature.

Satsuki azalea 'Kinsai'

Coast live oak

Here are key features to look for when shopping for broadleaf evergreens:

→ Small leaves

→ Interesting movement in the trunk

→ Attractive trunk with aged appearance

→ Good distribution of branches

→ Good surface roots

Bark on a cork oak

Yaupon holly

Tropical Bonsai

Many trees, shrubs, and vines that are native to the tropics are popular for bonsai, including ficus, jades, gardenias, and bougainvilleas.

Mature ficus trees have undulating trunks, impressive surface roots, and broad canopies. Many produce aerial roots that extend from the branches down to the soil.

Bougainvilleas and other vine bonsai may not have a characteristic mature shape, but they do have characteristic traits. When you're styling vines as bonsai, twist the trunks and branches to create movement that conveys a sense of how vines grow in nature.

Key Features to Develop

→ Surface roots. The roots of tropical bonsai grow near the surface to take advantage of nutrient-rich topsoil. Shallow containers can encourage lateral surface root growth.

→ Trunk and branches with sinuous movement. Branches on tropical bonsai grow in different directions to help them capture the best available light. Create this movement by wiring young trunks and branches.

→ Dense foliage. Sparse foliage on tropical bonsai indicates poor health and low light. Keeping tropical bonsai healthy will produce beautiful, dense leaves.

Willow leaf ficus

Here are key features to look for when shopping for tropicals:

→ Small leaves

→ Interesting movement in the trunk

→ Good distribution of branches

→ Good surface roots

→ Full, healthy leaves

Full, healthy leaves on a ficus

'Green Island' ficus

NEXT STEPS

In this chapter, I'll offer several starting points that can help you deepen your understanding of bonsai, build your skills, or get help with your trees. You'll also find suggestions for seeing beautiful bonsai in print or in person.

For an expanded and up-to-date version of this list, including links to related content and in-depth articles on the topics covered in this book, visit bonsaitonight.com/next-steps.

If you want help with your trees . . .

Take heart, because help is closer than you think. More than two hundred bonsai clubs and one hundred bonsai nurseries serve the bonsai community in the United States. A quick online search can determine the best options near you.

Bonsai clubs host workshops and meetings to help their members improve their trees. Meetings feature lectures on timely bonsai topics or demonstrations of specific techniques.

Bonsai nurseries are good places to find classes, trees, pots, tools, and supplies.

Subscribing to an online or print publication is a good way to learn new techniques or keep up with what's happening in the bonsai world. Here are some titles to check out:

→ *Bonsai Tonight*. My bonsai blog features detailed how-to articles for creating bonsai and photos from exhibits in the United States and Japan. bonsaitonight.com

→ *Bonsai: Journal of the American Bonsai Society*. This journal is known for publishing in-depth articles aimed at helping bonsai enthusiasts improve their trees. absbonsai.org

→ *International Bonsai* magazine. Each issue focuses on a specific topic such as maple bonsai or miniature bonsai and features articles translated from Japanese bonsai publications. internationalbonsai.com

Books and videos are great ways to learn bonsai, but they don't compare with hands-on experience. If the idea of studying with Japanese-trained bonsai professionals sounds good, the courses offered by the following organizations are a great next step:

→ Bonsai Boon offers multiday courses and streaming videos that feature basic techniques for popular species. bonsaiboon.com

- → Bonsai Mirai hosts multiday courses and weekly livestreams for students of all levels. bonsaimirai.com

- → Crataegus Bonsai offers seasonal multiday courses and an educational blog with tips on bonsai care and development. crataegus.com

- → Eisei-en hosts multiday courses and offers streaming videos for beginner, intermediate, and advanced bonsai students. eisei-en.com

If you want to see beautiful bonsai . . .

Seeing bonsai in person can inspire and educate. Many bonsai clubs host public exhibits, where members display their bonsai. You can also see beautiful bonsai in these gardens and exhibits:

Public Bonsai Gardens

- → Bonsai Collection at the Chicago Botanic Garden, Glencoe, Illinois. chicagobotanic.org/gardens/bonsai

- → Bonsai Collection at The Huntington, The Huntington Library, Art Collections, and Botanical Gardens, San Marino, California. gsbfhuntington.com

- → Bonsai Exhibit at the Smith Gilbert Gardens, Kennesaw, Georgia. smithgilbertgardens.com/at-the-gardens/bonsai-garden

- → Bonsai Exhibition Garden, North Carolina Arboretum, Asheville, North Carolina. ncarboretum.org/plan-a-visit/garden-exhibits/bonsai-exhibition-garden

- → Bonsai Garden at Lake Merritt, Lakeside Park, Oakland, California. bonsailakemerritt.com

- → C. V. Starr Bonsai Museum, Brooklyn Botanic Garden, Brooklyn, New York. bbg.org/collections/gardens/bonsai_museum

- → Clark Bonsai Collection, Shinzen Friendship Garden at Woodland Park, Fresno, California. gsbfclarkbonsaicollection.org

- → Dr. Ron and Arlene Kessler Bonsai Walk, Morikami Museum and Japanese Gardens, Delray Beach, Florida. morikami.org/roji-en/bonsai-collection

- → Elandan Gardens, Bremerton, Washington. elandangardens.com

- → Ellie M. Hill Bonsai Terrace, Portland Japanese Garden, Portland, Oregon. japanesegarden.org/garden-spaces/bonsai-terrace

- → James J. Smith Bonsai Gallery, Heathcote Botanical Gardens, Fort Pierce, Florida. heathcotebotanicalgardens.org/garden-rooms/james-j-smith-bonsai-gallery

- → Larz Anderson Collection of Japanese Dwarf Trees, Arnold Arboretum of Harvard University, Boston, Massachusetts. arboretum.harvard.edu/plants/featured-plants/bonsai

- → National Bonsai & Penjing Museum, US National Arboretum, Washington, DC. bonsai-nbf.org

- → Pacific Bonsai Museum, Federal Way, Washington. pacificbonsaimuseum.org

National Bonsai Exhibits

- → US National Bonsai Exhibition, Rochester, New York. The biennial event, hosted by William N. Valavanis, features an exhibit, demonstrations, critiques, lectures, and a large sales area. usnationalbonsai.com

- → US National Shohin Bonsai Exhibition, Kannapolis, North Carolina. The largest US show featuring small bonsai takes place every other year. The event includes an exhibit, workshops, demonstrations, and a sales area. internationalbonsai.com/page/493925678

The Bonsai Garden at Lake Merritt in Oakland, California

Bonsai in Japan

Japan is home to some of the world's top bonsai gardens. A good place to start is the Omiya Bonsai Village in Saitama, home to an outstanding bonsai museum and six well-known bonsai gardens. The museum features a rotating collection of world-class trees and educational displays. Historical gardens are within walking distance from the museum.

→ Omiya Bonsai Village: omiyabonsai.jp

→ Omiya Bonsai Art Museum: bonsai-art-museum.jp/en

Depending on when you visit, you may be able to attend a bonsai exhibition. The top two exhibitions are the Kokufu-ten and the Taikan-ten.

→ Kokufu-ten (National Exhibition). Japan's best-known bonsai exhibition takes place each February at the Tokyo Metropolitan

Art Museum in Ueno Park. More than two hundred displays feature some of the world's best bonsai. The nearby sales area offers an impressive selection of bonsai. bonsai-kyokai.or.jp/kokuhuten.htm (Japanese website)

→ Taikan-ten (Grand View Exhibition). Japan's top amateur exhibit takes place each November in Kyoto and features beautiful bonsai displays and a large sales area. facebook.com/nihonbonsaitaikanten

If you want to see beautiful photos of bonsai . . .

Bonsai photo books are a great way to get a sense of how different species can be styled. They are also a lot of fun to browse. Here are some of the best:

→ *U.S. National Bonsai Exhibition Commemorative Album*, by William N. Valavanis (International Bonsai, 2009–2019). These books, published biannually, feature photographs of some of the best bonsai in the United States, along with notes about the trees and the containers in which they grow. internationalbonsai.com/page/1442819

→ *Kokufu-ten Commemorative Album*, by Nippon Bonsai Association. Major bonsai exhibits in Japan produce commemorative albums featuring photographs of the trees on display. Albums from these exhibits, including the Kokufu-ten, Taikan-ten, and Gafu-ten, are available from online booksellers and auction sites (try searching for "Kokufu bonsai book"). Books in Japanese with limited English.

→ *In Training*, by Stephen Voss (Stephen Voss Photography, 2016). Photographs in this beautiful book by photographer Stephen Voss were shot over the course of one year at the National Bonsai & Penjing Museum in Washington, DC. Unlike the books listed above that feature photographs of trees and their containers, *In Training* focuses on detail shots that convey the experience of looking closely at beautiful bonsai. bonsaibook.net

If you want to find bonsai material . . .

If you're looking to expand your bonsai collection, you can acquire developed material or create new trees from scratch.

→ Bonsai nurseries are the obvious first stop when you're looking for developed trees. Some produce prebonsai trees that have good characteristics for bonsai but have not been fully styled. Other nurseries focus on more refined trees. Most retail bonsai nurseries are set up for shopping in person, but some have online storefronts and offer shipping.

→ Bonsai clubs commonly host auctions or sales in conjunction with their annual exhibits. These events are typically open to the public.

→ Retail nurseries or garden centers can be a great place to shop. Look for older material with low branches and interesting trunks. With proper care, many neglected nursery trees have the potential to become attractive bonsai.

→ Grow your own bonsai from a cutting or seed. Although this isn't the speediest route, it can be one of the most satisfying. For information about growing bonsai from seed or cutting, see bonsaitonight.com/next-steps.

ACKNOWLEDGMENTS

This book would not be possible without the people who made their trees available for photography: Boon Manakitivipart (page 91), Rick Trumm and Janet Nelson (page 74), Alexi Goranov (cover and pages 16-17, and 85), Rachel Hanson (pages 19 and 73; thanks, Mom!), Jeremiah Lee (pages 4 and 85), Bill Castellon (page 77), Eric Schrader (pages vi, 8, 11, 75, 79, 85, 88, 90, and 102), and the Bonsai Garden at Lake Merritt in Oakland, California (pages v, 8, 11, 93, 97, and 106). Special thanks to Bob Gould and Andrea Burhoe for coordinating the photo shoots at the garden.

Special thanks to David Fenton for the beautiful photography. Thanks to everyone at Ten Speed Press, especially managing editor Lisa Regul, for making this book a reality; Isabelle Gioffredi, for the beautiful design; and Dan Myers, for his production work. Thanks to Eric Schrader, Michael Hagedron and Lauren Takahashi for reading drafts of the book and providing feedback. Thanks to Daisaku Nomoto for styling the juniper in chapter III. Thanks to my father, Greg Dupuich, for instilling in me an appreciation of plants at a young age and continuing to support my work with small trees. Above all, thanks to Boon Manakitivipart for getting me started in bonsai and being an excellent teacher.

ABOUT THE AUTHOR

Jonas Dupuich runs a Northern California bonsai nursery where he teaches and writes about bonsai. He is the author of the *Bonsai Tonight* blog, a twice-weekly publication featuring how-to articles and photographs of bonsai around the world. His trees have been selected for display in local and regional exhibits, including the US National Bonsai Exhibition. Jonas grows a variety of different species and specializes in developing black pine bonsai from seed. Learn more at bonsaitonight.com.

Shimpaku juniper

INDEX

A

accent plants, 74, 75
ants, 34
aphids, 32, 33, 34, 36
azalea, satsuki, 87

B

bacteria, 36
bar branches, 44, 45
bonsai
  broadleaf evergreen, 86, 88
  caring for, 18, 20–21, 23–26, 28–37
  characteristics of, 6
  coniferous, 82, 84–85
  containers for, 60, 62–63, 65
  deciduous, 76, 78, 80–81
  definition of, 2
  displaying, 73–75
  etymology of, 2
  fertilizing, 29–31
  finding front of, 14–17
  material for, 99
  origins of, 5
  pests and diseases for, 31–37
  photo books of, 98–99
  places to see, 95–98
  selecting appropriate environment for, 20–21, 23–24
  styles of, 9–10, 12
  tropical, 89, 91
  watering, 24–26, 28
  See also techniques; *individual species*
bonsai clubs, 94, 99
bonsai nurseries, 94, 99
branch cutters, 40, 41
branch intersections, 44, 45
branch pads, 52, 84
branch ramification, 80
broadleaf evergreen bonsai, 86, 88
bunjin bonsai, 10

C

cascade bonsai, 9, 63
caterpillars, 34
chisels, 43
chopsticks, 42, 43
clubs, 94, 99
clump style bonsai, 10
coniferous bonsai, 82, 84–85
containers, 60, 62–63, 65
courses, 94–95
cut paste, 43

D

deciduous bonsai, 76, 78, 80–81
diseases, 31–32, 36–37
display, 73–75
dormancy, 26
driftwood style bonsai, 10

E

elm
  cork bark Chinese, 75, 79
  gray-bark, vi
exposed root bonsai, 12

powdery mildew, 35, 36
pruning, 43, 45–47
publications, 94
pussy willow, dwarf, 65

Q

quince, dwarf Japanese, 64, 81

R

redwood, coast, v, 8, 106
repotting, 67–72
root cutters, 42
root hooks, 42, 43
root-over-rock bonsai, 12
root rakes, 42, 43
root rot, 36
rust, 36

S

scale, 32, 33, 34, 36
scissors, 40, 41
semi-cascade bonsai, 9, 63
shari, 10, 15, 43
sickles, 42
slant style bonsai, 9
slugs, 34
snails, 34
soil, 71
sooty mold, 32, 33, 36
spider mites, 33, 34
spruce, 8
stewartia, 11
styles, 9–10, 12
sunlight, 20, 23–24

T

Taikan-ten, 97–98
techniques
    pruning, 43, 45–47
    repotting, 67–72
    step-by-step demonstration of, 56–59
    wiring, 48, 50–54
    See also tools
temperature, 24
thrips, 33, 34
tools
    basic, 40–41
    specialized, 42–43
    sterilizing, 37
triple-trunk bonsai, 10
tropical bonsai, 89, 91
tweezers, 40, 41
twin-trunk bonsai, 10

W

watering, 24–26, 28
whiteflies, 32
whorls, 44, 45
windswept bonsai, 10
wire cutters, 40, 41
wiring, 48, 50–54
wisteria, dwarf, 81

Y

yamadori bonsai, 10

Published in the United States by Ten Speed Press,
an imprint of Random House, a division of
Penguin Random House LLC, New York.
www.tenspeed.com

Ten Speed Press and the Ten Speed Press
colophon are registered trademarks of
Penguin Random House LLC.

Library of Congress Cataloging-in-Publication Data
Names: Dupuich, Jonas, 1971- author.
Title: The little book of bonsai / An Easy Guide
 to Caring for Your Bonsai Tree Jonas Dupuich;
 Photographs by David Fenton
Description: First Edition | Emeryville, CA Ten Speed
 Press 2020. | Summary: "The perfect gift for any
 new bonsai owner, this charming, compact, beautifully
 photographed beginner's guide to bonsai from expert
 Jonas Dupuich covers all the basics to keep your
 bonsai alive and happy"—Provided by publisher.
Identifiers: LCCN 2019020462 | ISBN 9780399582592
 (hardcover) | ISBN 9780399582608 (ebook)
Subjects: LCSH: Bonsai.
Classification: LCC SB433.5 .D87 2020 | DDC
 635.9/772—dc23
LC record available at https://lccn.loc.gov/2019020462

Hardcover ISBN: 978-0-399-58259-2
eBook ISBN: 978-0-399-58260-8

Printed in China

Design by Isabelle Gioffredi

10 9 8 7 6

First Edition

Coast redwood